Beginner's Guide to Python

Table of Contents

Chapter 1
Overview

Python is an object-oriented scripting language invented by Guido van Russom in 1991. Being a general-purpose programming language, it is widely used in many applications today across various domains such as ***scientific computing, desktop applications, web applications, etc. It is an interpreted language***, meaning there is a Python Interpreter which executes Python programs line by line as opposed to compiled languages wherein the entire program is compiled into executable code.

One of the major advantages of Python is that it is a cross-platform language with interpreters available for every major Operating System out there; namely ***Windows, Linux, MAC, FreeBSD, etc.*** A single Python program can be executed across any platform regardless of the Operating System and the Hardware Architecture as long as a suitable interpreter is present and the program is free from platform-specific code. Another major advantage is the design philosophy that emphasizes on code readability and a syntax that enables developers to implement concepts in fewer lines of code as compared to languages like C++, Java or C#.

Several Python implementations exist for different operating systems today. CPython is the reference implementation written C, also happens to be the most used one. Some of the other major implementations are – ***IronPython (for .NET and Mono framework) and Jython (written in Java).***

1.1 Potential of Python

As of 2017, Python is in great demand and also widely used in the IT industry. Some of the applications where Python is used include Internet of ***Things (IoT), BigData, Cloud Computing, Machine Learning, etc.*** In fact, some of the devices, applications or services you use could be powered by Python to some degree. To name a few – ***YouTube, DropBox, Quora, BitTorrent and Yahoo Maps*** use Python somewhere or the other in their systems. This goes to show how incredibly useful and powerful is Python.

Chapter 2
Installation and Environment Setup

There are two versions of Python in use today – Python 2 and Python 3. While Python 2 is more common, Python 3 is relatively newer. There is a fair bit of difference in both the versions with respect to syntax. This guide focuses only on Python 2. The programs demonstrated in this book have been tested on Windows 8 and shall seamlessly work on MAC OS and Linux unless specified otherwise.

If you use MAC OS or Unix/Linux based OS, you will mostly have Python shipped along with your OS. In order to check, open the ***Terminal/Shell*** and type the following command:

$>python

If this command returns an error with the likes of "command not found", "invalid file or directory" or something similar then Python is most likely not present on your system. If no error is returned, a ***Python Shell*** will open which will prove the existence of Python interpreter on your system.

On Windows systems, Python is not shipped by default and you will have to install it manually.

2.1 Downloading and Installing Python

If Python is not present on your system regardless of the OS, you will have to download and install it. To do so, visit: https://www.python.org/downloads/ and chose the appropriate

Python 2.x installation file in accordance with your Operating System and Hardware Architecture. For eg. If you have a 64-bit Windows OS, the right file will be - python-2.7.12.amd64.msi, 2.7.13 is the Python version and amd64 is a notation for 64-bit architecture. The same for a 32-bit Windows OS is 2.7.12.msi. Always get the latest version. Once the file has been downloaded, execute it and follow the instructions. While installing, the setup will give you an option to customize Python. The option "Add python.exe to Path" will be unchecked by default, click on the icon next to it and enable the option as shown below. Click Next and finish the installation.

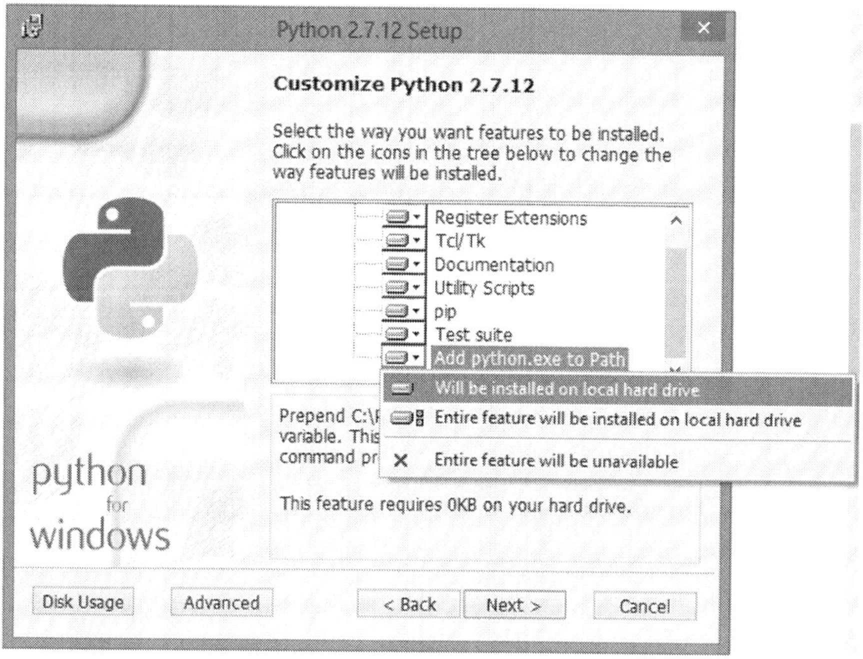

Once the installation is complete, open command prompt (cmd.exe) and type the following:

C:\> python

A ***Python Shell*** will open which will look more or less like the following:

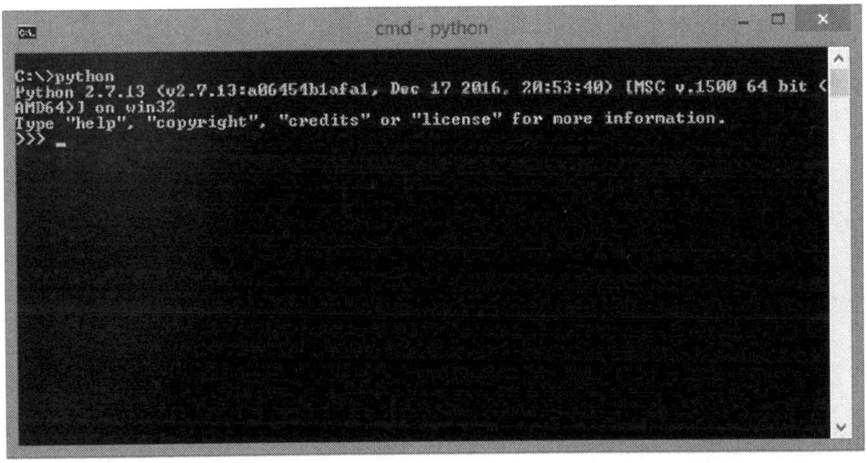
cmd - python
C:\>python
Python 2.7.13 (v2.7.13:a06454b1afa1, Dec 17 2016, 20:53:40) [MSC v.1500 64 bit (
AMD64)] on win32
Type "help", "copyright", "credits" or "license" for more information.
>>>

If you are able to open Python Shell, Python has been successfully installed on your system.

Chapter 3
Introduction to Python Programming

Python offers two modes of programming:

- **Interactive Mode:**

In this mode, the Python Interpreter (also known as Python Shell) is launched without passing a script to it. In MAC/Linux, you can just type ***python*** in the terminal/shell and in Windows, type ***python*** in the command prompt as mentioned in the previous section. A GUI shell called IDLE (Python's Integrated DeveLopment Environment) is supplied with the Windows distribution of Python which is just a shell with different looks and added features. Once the Python Interpreter is opened, you can interact with it using Python commands. Let us consider the command ***print*** which is used to display text on the screen. Type the following statement and press enter:

>>> *print "Hello World!"*

The output will look like:

Hello World!

Interactive Mode lets us enter one command at a time. This is well suited for trying out small code snippets, debugging and carrying out small tasks in general.

- **Script Mode:**

  A Python script is passed as a parameter to the Python interpreter which executes the script line by line. Let us write a very simple Python script with ***the print*** command. To do so, open a text editor such as Notepad, type:

  print "Hello World!"

  On the first line and save the file as *hello.py*. Note that ***.py*** is the extension for Python scripts. Open command prompt, navigate to the directory where hello.py has been saved and enter the following command:

  C:\> python hello.py

  The output will look like:

  Hello World!

  In the above example, the Python Interpreter is invoked and "*hello.py*" script is passed to it as a parameter. The interpreter starts executing each command from the script, in this case, *print "Hello World!"* is the only command, thus *Hello World!* Is displayed on the screen.

3.1 Writing Python Scripts

You will be using script mode programming most of the times. In general, Python scripts are written in text editors. Choosing a text editor that suits your needs is important. On Windows, ***Notepad++*** is a good text editor, well suited for Python Programming. On Linux, the default editors such as ***emacs, vi,***

gedit and kwrite do a great job. ***TextEdit*** on MAC will do the job just fine.

On Linux, MAC and other Unix-like operating systems, the first line of the script should be the ***shebang line***. Shebang is a character sequence of a hash symbol followed by an exclamation mark *(#!)* at the start of the script. Using a shebang line is a standard procedure for most scripting languages such as ***Python, Perl, Ruby, Bash/Shell***. It tells the script which interpreter to use. The general syntax for a shebang is:

#!<interpreter> <arguments>

For Python, it is:

#!/usr/bin/python or *#!/usr/bin/env python*

Using *#!/usr/bin/env python* is a better and a safer option as env automatically looks up the Python Interpreter's path. Note that Windows does not have shebang support and hence a shebang line is not needed while writing Python scripts on Windows. Once a script is written, it is saved as *<script name>.py*.

3.2 Executing Python Scripts

- **Windows:**

Open ***command prompt (cmd.exe)***, navigate to the folder where the script has been saved by using the ***cd*** command. If you are totally new to using the command prompt, it is a good idea to do learn a few basic DOS commands. Once you have navigated to the folder where the script is present, type the following command and press enter:

C:\> python <script name>.py

If the script name is *xyz.py*, the above command will look like:

C:\> python xyz.py

- **Linux/MAC:**

Open Terminal/Shell, navigate to the folder where the script has been saved by using the ***cd*** command. Like DOS commands in Windows, having the basic knowledge of Shell/Bash commands on Linux/MAC will help immensely. Once you are in the concerned directory, there are two ways of executing a Python file.

1. **Making the Python Script executable:**

In Linux, MAC and other Unix-Like operating systems, a file can have read, write and execute permissions. To edit permissions of a file, chmod command is used. A full explanation of chmod and file permissions is beyond the scope of this book and hence only the required details will be explained. In order to make a script executable, the following command is used:

$>chmod +x <script name>.py

If the script name is *xyz.py*, the above command will look like:

$>chmod +x xyz.py

The option "+x" is used to make a script executable. To execute the script, use the following command:

$>./<script name>.py

If the script name is *xyz.py*, the above command will look like:

$>./xyz.py

<u>Note</u>: This method makes a script standalone executable. The script will know which interpreter to use from the ***shebang line***. If the shebang line is incorrect, the script will fail to execute.

2. **Invoking Python Interpreter:**

   In this method, you invoke the Python interpreter and pass the script as a parameter. To do so, use the following command:

   $>python <script name>.py

   If the script name is *xyz.py*, the above command will look like:

   $> python xyz.py

   This method will work even without the file having execute permissions and without a shebang line. However, it is always a good practice to include a shebang line.

3.3 Basic Syntax

3.3.1 Identifiers

A name used to identify a variable, function, module, class or any other object is known as an identifier. An identifier name starts with an alphabet or an underscore (_). Digits can be present inside an identifier name but cannot start with one. Special characters such as @, #, %, etc. cannot be part of identifier names. Python is case sensitive which means identifiers ebook and eBook will be treated as two different names.

3.3.2 Keywords

Python Keywords are reserved words which cannot be used as variables or identifiers. Keywords are always lower case strings. Below is a list of all the keywords in alphabetical order:

and	exec	not
assert	finally	or
break	for	pass
class	from	print
continue	global	raise
def	if	return
del	import	try
elif	in	while
else	is	with
except	lambda	yield

Each keyword has a specific function; the basic ones are covered in this book.

3.3.3 Code Format

Every line is considered as one statement in Python. You can have multiple statements on one line, each one of them separated by a semicolon (;). A semicolon is not needed otherwise to indicate the end of a statement.

For example, consider the following code:

print "Hi, this is a python tutorial"

print "Multi-line statements are demonstrated here"

There are two print statements, one on each line. This can also be written as:

print "Hi, this is a python tutorial"; print "Multi-line statements are demonstrated here"

Although there is a choice to put multiple statements on one line, it is a standard practice to put one statement on one line. A single statement can also be written across multiple lines using the continuation character (\) as follows:

*print "Hello *

*This shows the *

*usage of *

continuation character"

The above print statement is the same as:

print "Hello This shows the usage of continuation character"

Python does not have the concept of braces to indicate a code block. A block in Python is indicated by a tab-space indent. The following images will make the indentation concept clearer:

```
1  print "This is indentation demo"
2  x = 5
3  y = 5
4  if ( x == y ):
5      print "Indented block executes..."
6      print "Another statement in the same block executes..."
7  print "This statement does not come under the indented block..."
8  
```

In the code shown above, there is an "*if*" statement on Line No. 4. Whichever statements we want to include inside the "*if*" block are preceded by 1 tab-space on each line. As seen, there are two print statement inside the "*if*" block, on line 5 and 6. You do not have to understand how "**if**" statement works in order to understand indentation. Detailed explanation on how if statements and other control structures work are given in the further sections of this book.

The code in the following image shows the wrong example of code blocks:

```
print "This is indentation demo"
x = 5
y = 5
if ( x == y ):
print "This is not inside the if block..."
print "This syntax is not correct..."
print "The interpreter will return an error..."
```

None of the statements after the "if" statement are preceded by 1 tab-space indent. The interpreter will not know which statements are to be executed inside the "if" block. The above code will throw an error.

A code block can also be nested inside another code block as shown below:

indent.py

```
1  print "This is indentation demo"
2  x = 5
3  y = 5
4  if ( x == y ):
5      print "This is the first if block.."
6      if ( x > 2 ):
7          print "This is the second if block.."
8          if ( y < 8 ):
9              print "This is the third if block.."
10
```

There are 3 "if" statements on line 4, 6 and 8. "If" statement on line 8 comes inside the block of "if" statement of line 6 which in-turn comes under the block of "if" statement present on line 4. As the level of nested code blocks increases, the tab spaces from the baseline also increase.

3.3.4 Comments

A comment is a line that will be skipped by the interpreter at the time of execution. In Python, there are single line as well as multi-line comments. Single line comments start with hash (#) symbol. For example:

#This is a single line comment

Multi-line comments are enclosed between 3 single quotes ('") as follows:

'''

This is line 1 of multi-line comments

This is line 2

And this is line 3

'''

3.3.5 Quotes

Quotes are used to denote strings in Python. Single ('), double (") and triple ('" or """) quotes are supported. Usually, single quote is used for a word and double quotes are used for a sentence. Multi-line strings can be denoted only using triple quotes.

print 'word'

print "This is a sentence"

print '''This is a multi-line string

Enclosed within trip quotes'''

There is no need to use continuation character (\) as mentioned in section 3.3.3 if using triple quotes to denote multi-line strings.

3.3.6 User Input

A function called ***raw_input*** is used to wait for user's input. When the interpreter comes across this function, the execution is blocked until the user enters something. The general syntax of this function is:

<variable> = raw_input("<Message to be displayed while waiting for input>")

Whatever input is given by the user will be returned by the ***raw_input*** function and stored in <variable>. The content of this variable will always be in string format regardless of what is entered by the user. You will more about variables and data types in the following sections of the book.

Chapter 4
Variables

Variables are identifiers used to store data. In Python, variables are generic in nature, meaning there is no data type for variables. The same variable can be used to store numbers, strings or any other type of data at different times. When a variable is created, some location in the memory is reserved to store the content of the variable.

Declaration of a variable is not required; it happens implicitly when assigning a value to a variable. To assign a value, equal to sign (=) is used. The variable should be to the left of the equal to sign and the value to be assigned should be to the right. For example:

x = 50

y = 75.4

name = "Chad"

x is assigned an integer value of 50, **y** is assigned a floating point value of 75.4 and **name** is assigned a string "Chad". As seen from this example, it is clear that the syntax remains the same across all data types.

Multiple assignment is also possible as follows:

x = y = z = 100

This statement will assign 100 to x, y, and z.

Another way of using multiple assignment is:

x, y, name = 80.8, 41, "eBook"

This statement is equivalent to:

x = 80.8

y = 41

name = "eBook"

4.1 Standard Data Types

Python has standard data types for storing different kinds of data. For example, a name is of string type and weight is of numerical type. The standard data types are:

- Numbers
- Strings
- Lists
- Tuples
- Dictionary

4.1.1 Numbers

Number data types are used to store numeric values. This datatype can be further divided into the following sub-datatypes:

- int (Signed Integers)
- long (Long Integers)
- float (Floating point values)

- complex (Complex Numbers)

Here are some examples of each type:

int

x = 45

y = 87

long

a = 458393L

b = -27654324L

float

c = 16.98

d = 0.0

complex

x = 5.67j

y = 4 + 20j

4.1.2 Strings

A string is a continuous set of characters within quotation marks. Python supports single, double and triple quotes. While single and double quotes are normally used, triple quotes are used to denote multi-line strings. The slice operator ([ ] and [:]) is used to take sub-strings from a string. Concatenation operator (+) is used to join two strings. The following examples show basic string operations:

Consider a string variable ***str***, with content ***"Hello Python"***

str = "Hello Python"

String indexes start at 0 at the beginning of the string, end at -1. Check out the following piece of code and read the comments (starting with #) to understand how basic string operations work:

str[0] #Will return the first character of the string which is ***H***

str[-1] #Will return the last character of the string which is **n**

str[1:4] #Will return character sequence from 1 to 4 which is **ello**

str[2:] #Will return character sequence from 2 till the end which is ***llo Python***

message = str + " World" #Concatenate **World** *to str which has a value* ***of Hello Python*** *and assign to the variable message. The contents of the variable message will be* ***Hello Python World***

4.1.3 Lists

A list is a collection of items of same or different data type. Items of a list are enclosed within square brackets ([ ]) and separated by a comma. Contents of the list can be accessed using the slice operator ([ ] and [:]). Index starts at 0 and ends at -1. Concatenation operator (+) is used to join lists.

Consider the following lists:

list1 = ['apple', 68, 56, 'football', 23.98, 'car']

list2 = [120, 'cat', 8.9]

Go through the following code and comments in order to understand how operations on lists are performed:

list1 [0] #Will return the first item of the list which is **apple** *(string)*

list2[1:] #Will return a sub-list of elements from 1 till the end of list2 which is

 # ['cat', 8.9]

list1 [2:4] #Will return a sub list of items from 2 to 4 of list1 which is

 # [56, 'football', 23.98]

*list3 = list1 + list2 #**list2** will be concatenated to **list1** and assigned to a new variable*

*# **list3**. The contents of **list3** will be*

 # ['apple', 68, 56, 'football', 23.98, 'car', 120, 'cat', 8.9]

4.1.4 Tuples

A tuple is a collection of items of same or different datatypes, similar to a list. However, a tuple is enclosed in parenthesis (( )) instead of square brackets ([ ]). A tuple can be considered as a read-only list as elements and size of a list can be changed but a tuple cannot be edited once initialized.

Consider the following tuples:

tuple1 = (3, 5.6, 'eBook', 98, 'World')

tuple2 = (183, 'Hello')

Go through the following code and comments in order to understand how operations on tuples are performed:

tuple1[0] #Will return the first element of ***tuple1*** *which is* ***3***

tuple1[1:3] #Will return a tuple containing items from 1 to 3 of ***tuple1****, that is*

***(5.6, 'eBook', 98)***

tuple1[2:] #Will return a tuple containing items of tuple1 from 2 till the end,

 # Which is ***('eBook', 98, 'World')***

tuple3 = tuple1 + tuple2 #Concatenate tuple1 and tuple2 and assign to tuple3.

 # tuple3 will now look like ***(3, 5.6, 'eBook', 98, 'World', 183, 'Hello')***

4.1.5 Dictionary

A dictionary is a datatype that consists of a key-value pair. It works like a look-up table with the key being the index. A key can be of any datatype (usually strings and numbers are used) and has to be unique. Curly brackets ({ }) are used to enclose the contents of a dictionary. The standard syntax is:

Dict = { <key>:<value> }

For example:

dict = { 1 : 'one' , 'Toronto' : 'Canada', 'Florida' : 'USA' , 'Six' : 6 }

Values can be assigned or accessed using square brackets ([ ]) as shown below:

dict[1] #Will return the value of ***Key 1*** *which is* ***'one'*** *dict['Florida'] #Will return the value of* ***Key 'Florida'*** *which is* ***'USA'***

dict['Apple'] = 'Fruit' #Will create a new ***Key called 'Apple'*** *and assign a string value of* ***'Fruit'*** *to it.*

dict['Toronto'] = 'Ontario' #Will update ***'Toronto' Key's*** *value to* ***'Ontario'***

An empty dictionary can also be initialized and assigned values later as follows:

dict = { }

dict[5] = 'Five' #Will create a ***Key 5*** *and assign string value of* ***'Five'*** *to it.*

dict['Tomato'] = 'Vegetable' #Will create a ***Key 'Tomato'*** *and assign a string value of* ***'Vegetable'*** *to it.*

There are two functions called ***keys()*** and ***values()*** which can be used to retrieve all keys and values from a dictionary respectively. These functions return the values in the form of a list. The standard syntax is:

dict.keys() #Returns all keys of the dictionary dict as a list

dict.values() #Returns all values of the dictionary dict as a list

4.2 Data Type Conversion

Python offers standard functions for converting one data type to another. Not all datatypes can be converted into all other datatypes and some functions will lose some data like floating point precision in case of floating point to integer conversion.

Below is a table that contains standard datatype conversion functions and their description:

Function	Description
int(x [,base])	Converts x to an integer. x can be anything – string, float, etc. If x is a float, this function may lose the precision. base specifies the base if x is a string.
float(x)	Converts x to a floating-point number. x can be anything – string, int, etc.
long(x [,base])	Converts x to a long integer. x can be anything – string, float, etc. base specifies the base if x is a string.
complex(real [,imag])	Creates a complex number. real is the real part and imag is the imaginary part.
str(x)	Converts x to string. x can be anything – int, float, long, etc.
repr(x)	Converts x to an expression string.
eval(str)	Evaluates a string and returns an object.
list(s)	Converts s to a list.
tuple(s)	Converts s to a tuple.
dict(d)	Creates a dictionary. d must be a sequence of (key,value) tuples.
set(s)	Converts to a set.
frozenset(s)	Converts s to a frozen set.
chr(x)	Converts x (integer) to a character based on ASCII.
unichr(x)	Converts x (integer) to a Unicode character.
ord(x)	Converts x (single character) to its integer value, based on ASCII.
hex(x)	Converts x (integer) to a hexadecimal string.
oct(x)	Converts x (integer) to an octal string.

4.3 Sample Program

Here is a sample program containing some of the concepts covered so far. Copy the program to your text editor, save the file with *.py* extension. Open command prompt (cmd.exe), navigate to the directory where the file has been saved and run the script with the command – ***python <filename>.py***. For more details on script execution and running the script on other Operating Systems, go back to section 3.1.

```
#Sample Program with concepts from user input, strings, etc.

#Print a welcome message. '\n' is the new line character

print "Welcome, some of the concepts covered so far will be demonstrated in this program. \n"

#Prompt user input for First Name

first_name = raw_input("Enter your first name: ")

#Prompt user input for Last Name

last_name = raw_input("Enter your last name: ")

#Prompt user input for Age

age = raw_input("Enter your age: ")

#Display all the input values with string concatenation

print "\n\nYour name is " + first_name + " " + last_name + " and you are " + age + " years old.\n"

#raw_input function always returns a string value regardless of what is entered

#age variable will have string value, convert it to int

age_integer = int (age)

#Create Dictionary with users details

user_dict = { "FirstName": first_name , "LastName": last_name, "Age": age_integer }

print "\n\nUsers details in dictionary:\n"

print user_dict
```

Output:

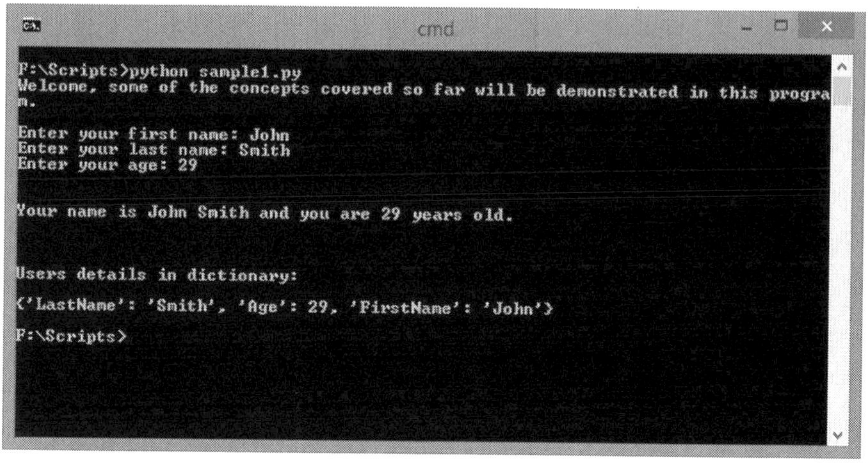
cmd
F:\Scripts>python sample1.py
Welcome, some of the concepts covered so far will be demonstrated in this progra
m.
Enter your first name: John
Enter your last name: Smith
Enter your age: 29
Your name is John Smith and you are 29 years old.
Users details in dictionary:
{'LastName': 'Smith', 'Age': 29, 'FirstName': 'John'}
F:\Scripts>

The above code makes use of some of the concepts covered so far. Comments are placed before key statements which explain what a particular statement does.

Chapter 5
Operators

Operators are constructs which behave generally like functions, but which differ syntactically or semantically from usual functions. Python operators are used to manipulate and compare operands.

Python supports the following types of operators:

- Arithmetic Operators
- Comparison Operators
- Assignment Operators
- Logical Operators
- Bitwise Operators
- Membership Operators
- Identity Operators

5.1 Arithmetic Operators

Arithmetic Operators are used to perform arithmetic operations on the operands. Consider 3 operands – a = 10, b = 20, c = 30. Each of the arithmetic operators are explained with the help of these operands

5.1.1 Addition (+)

Adds values on either side of the operator. Eg. a + b = 30

5.1.2 Subtraction (-)

Subtracts operand on the right from the left. Eg. a – b = -10

5.1.3 Multiplication (*)

Multiplies operands on either side of the operator. Eg. b * c = 600

5.1.4 Division (/)

Divides operand on the left by the operand on the right. Eg. c / a = 3

5.1.5 Modulus (%)

Returns remainder after dividing the operand on the left with the operand on the right. Eg. 3 % 2 = 1

5.1.6 Exponent (**)

Raises the exponential power of the operand on the left to the value of the operand on the right. Eg. 2 ** 5 = 32 (Equivalent to $2^5 = 32$)

5.1.7 Floor Division (//)

This operator is the mathematical floor function. The right operand divides the left one and a quotient is assigned obtained. This quotient is then rounded off to the nearest integer less than or equal to the quotient. Eg. 5 // 2 = 2 (Original quotient 2.5 is rounded off to 2 as 2 is less than 2.5); -5/2 = -3 (Original quotient -2.5 is rounded off to -3 as -3 is less than -2.5)

5.2 Comparison Operators

Comparison operators are used to compare operands on either side of the operator. The operation results in a Boolean True or False value. Consider 3 operands – a = 10, b = 20. These operands will be used to demonstrate the working of comparison operators as follows:

5.2.1 Equal-to (==)

Returns True if operands on either side of the operator are equal, returns False otherwise. Eg. (a == b) will return False.

5.2.2 Not Equal-to (!=)

Returns True if operands on either side of the operator are not equal, returns False otherwise. Eg. (a != b) will return False.

5.2.3 Less-than (<)

Returns True if the left operand is less than the operand on the right, returns false if the operand on the right is greater than the operand on the left. Eg. (a < b) will return True.

5.2.4 Greater-than (>)

Returns True if the left operand is greater than the operand on the right, returns false if the operand on the right is less than the operand on the left. Eg. (a > b) will return False.

5.2.5 Less-than or Equal-to (<=)

Returns True if the left operand is less than or equal to the operand on the right, returns false if the operand on the right is greater than the operand on the left. Eg. (a <= b) will return True.

5.2.6 Greater-than or Equal-to (>=)

Returns True if the left operand is greater than or equal to the operand on the right, returns false if the operand on the right is less than the operand on the left. Eg. (a >= b) will return False.

5.3 Assignment Operators

Assignment Operators are used to assign values to variables. In Python, there is a normal assignment operator and there are various types of compound assignment operators. We shall take a look at each one of them.

5.3.1 Assignment (=)

This is the basic assignment operator which assigns value of the operand on the right to the operand on the left. Eg. a = b

5.3.2 Add and Assign (+=)

This operator adds the value of the operand on the right to the operand on the left and the sum is then assigned to the operand on the left. Eg. a+=b is the same as a = a + b

5.3.3 Subtract and Assign (-=)

The right operand will be subtracted from the left one and the resulting value will be assigned to the left operand. Eg. a-=b is the same as a = a - b

5.3.4 Multiply and Assign (*=)

This operator multiplies both the operands and the product is then assigned to the operand on the left. Eg. a*=b is the same as a = a * b

5.3.5 Divide and Assign (/=)

The right operand will divide the left one and the quotient will be assigned to the left operand. Eg. a/=b is the same as a = a / b

5.3.6 Modulus and Assign (%=)

The right operand will divide the left one and the remainder of the division will be assigned to the left operand. Eg. a%=b is the same as a = a % b

5.3.7 Exponent and Assign (**=)

This operator will raise the exponential power of the left operand by a value of the right operand and assign the result to the left operand. Eg. a**=b is the same as a = a ** b

5.3.8 Floor Divide and Assign (//=)

The right operand will floor-divide the left one and the quotient will be assigned to the left operand. Eg. a//=b is the same as a = a // b

5.4 Bitwise Operators

Bitwise operators carry out operations at a bit level on the operands. This happens at a bit by bit binary level.

Consider these two operators a = 40 and b = 75 which are equivalent to a = 00101000 and b = 01001011 in binary. These operands will be used to explain the working of bitwise operators as follows:

5.4.1 Bitwise Binary AND (&)

Performs binary AND on operands bit by bit. The resulting bit is 1 only if both the bits of the operands is 1. Eg. a & b = 00001000

5.4.2 Bitwise Binary OR (|)

Performs binary OR on operands bit by bit. The resulting bit is 1 if at least one of the bits of the operands is 1. Eg. a | | b = 01101011

5.4.3 Bitwise Binay XOR (^)

Performs binary XOR. The resulting bit is 1 only if either of the bits of the operands is 1 but not both. Eg. a ^ b = 01100011

5.4.4 Bitwise Binary Inversion (~)

This is a unary operator. Performs binary inversion. Takes binary 2's complement, inverts the sign. General formula -- ~n = - (n – 1). Eg. ~a = -0111101 (-41 in decimal)

5.4.5 Binary Left Shift (<<)

This operator shifts bits to the left of the operand on the left by the number of places specified by the operand on the right. Eg. a << 2 = 10100000

5.4.6 Binary Right Shift (>>)

This operator shifts bits to the right of the operand on the left by the number of places specified by the operand on the right. Eg. a >> 2 = 00001010

5.4 Logical Operators

Python offers 3 logical operators mainly used for decision making and looping but also has other uses. These operators return a Boolean Value True or False.

5.4.1 Logical AND (and)

Performs logical AND on operands. The result is True if both the operands are True. Eg. (True and True) = True, (True and False) = False.

5.4.2 Logical OR (or)

Performs logical OR on operands. The result is True if one of the operands is True. Eg. (True and False) = True, (False and False) = False.

5.4.3 Logical NOT (not)

This is a unary operator. Performs logical inversion of the operand. Eg. (not True) = False, (not False) = True.

5.5 Membership Operators

Python offers two membership operators to test membership in a sequence object such as string, list, tuple, and dictionary. These operators return a Boolean Value True or False.

Consider the following variables:

str = "This is membership operator demo" #String

list1 = [1, 50.0, "Python", 25] #List

dict1 = ["Toronto" : "Canada", 7: "Seven", "Ten" : 10] #Dictionary

Their variables will be used to demonstrate the working of membership operators.

5.5.1 in Operator (in)

Returns True if the given object is present in the sequence, False otherwise. Eg:

"demo" in str = True as "demo" is present in str

80 in list1 = False as 80 is not present list1

"Toronto" in dict1 = True as "Toronto" is a key present in dict1

"Canada" in dict1 = False – Although "Canada" is present as a value somewhere in dict1, it is not a key.

5.5.2 not in Operator (not in)

Returns True if the given object is not present in the sequence, False otherwise. Eg:

“operator” not in str = False as “operator” is present in srt

80 not in list1 = True as 80 is not present in list1

“Ten” not in dict1 = False as “Ten” is present as a key in dict1.

5.6 Identity Operators

Identity operators provide a way of comparing variables, objects or types. These are usually used to determine if a variable or an object is of a certain type. Consider the following variables:

a = 5 #int

b = 7.5 #float

In order to find the type of a variable, the built-in function type() is used. Eg. ***type(a)*** will return ***type int*** and ***type(b)*** will return ***type float.*** These variables and the type() will be used to explain identity operators as follows:

5.6.1 is Operator (is)

Returns True if both the operands are the same in type or value.

Eg. a is 5 = True, type(b) is float = True.

5.6.2 is not Operator (is not)

Returns True if both the operands are not the same in type or value.

Eg. b is not 5.3 = True, type(a) is not int = False.

Chapter 6
Control Structures

A control structure is a block of code which analyses the given condition based on certain parameters and decides a direction in which to go. Python offers selection and iteration based control structures where selection is decision making and iteration based control structures are loops in simple terms. We will cover each of these.

6.1 Decision Making

Decision making deals with executing certain code block based on certain conditions. A condition is nothing but an expression that evaluates to True or False. All non-zero and non-null values are assumed as True and all zero and null values are assumed as false. These structures indicate a code block and hence all the statements under them should come at a tab space indent. Things will be clearer once you take a look at the example; for now, let us look at the different decision making options available.

6.1.1 *if* Statement

The *if* statement is the de-facto requirement of a decision-making block. The block containing an *if* statement will get activated if the stated condition becomes true. General syntax:

```
if ( <condition> ):
Statement 1
```

Statement 2

...

As seen from the syntax, the ***if*** statement has been supplied with a condition. If that condition evaluates to True, statements under it will be executed. Also seen from the syntax is that the statements under the ***if*** statement are at a tab space indent.

Example:

x = 20

if (x > 10):

print "if block executed"

In the above example, x is a variable which holds a value of 20. The condition for the ***if*** block to get activated is (x > 10). We know that 20 > 10, the condition will evaluate to True and hence this block will get activated which means the print statement under the block will get executed. If x was not greater than 10, the condition would evaluate to False and the block would not get activated.

6.1.2 *elif* Statement

elif is short for Else-If. This statement can only be present if there is a preceding ***if*** statement in the same code block, i.e You cannot have a standalone ***elif*** statement. The execution will reach the ***elif*** statement if and only if the conditions of the preceding if or elif statements within the same code block evaluate to False. Like the ***if*** statement, ***elif*** statement also needs a condition. An ***elif***

block will get activated if the supplied condition evaluates to True. General Syntax:

```
if (<condition>):

Statements...

elif (<condition>):

Statements...
```

Example:

```
x = 50

if ( x > 50 ):

print "x > 75, if block executed"

elif ( x == 50 ):

print "x = 50, elif block executed"
```

In the above example, the variable x has a value of 50. Once the execution control reaches the ***if*** statement, x > 50 condition will be evaluated. The result will be false as x is not greater than 50. The control will then jump to the ***elif*** statement and evaluate its condition x == 50. The result of this evaluation will be true and hence the statements inside the ***elif*** block will be executed. Had the condition of the ***if*** statement evaluated to True, the execution control would have skipped all the ***elif*** statements present in the same code block (in this example, only one).

6.1.3 *else* Statement

The ***else*** statement is not a standalone statement and requires a preceding ***if*** statement in the same code block. Unlike the ***if*** and the ***elif*** statements, no condition is required for the else statement. An ***else*** code block will get executed if and only if the conditions of all the preceding ***if*** and ***elif*** (in case they are present) statements evaluate to false. General Syntax:

if <condition>:

Statements…

else:

Statements…

Example:

x = 30

if (x == 10):

print "x = 10, if block executed…"

else:

print "x is not equal to 10, else block executed…"

A variable x has been initialized to 30. When the execution control will reach ***if (x == 10)***, the condition will evaluate to False as x is not equal to 10. If there were ***elif*** blocks in this code, the control would have jumped to each one of those statements to evaluate their condition but since they are not present in this example, the control will jump straight to the else statement thereby activating the block and executing all the statements inside the ***else*** block.

You can have multiple ***elif*** statements in the same code block to check for multiple conditions. It is even possible to nest decision-making blocks inside other decision-making blocks. The three important things to remember here are:

1. All statements under ***if/elif/else*** should come at ***one tab-space indent*** as they represent ***code blocks***.
2. ***elif and else*** statements are ***not standalone*** statements and require preceding ***if*** statement.
3. ***if*** and ***elif*** statements need to be supplied with a condition whereas ***else*** statement cannot be given a condition to evaluate.

6.2 Loops

Statements in a script are executed one after the other. At times, there may be a need to execute a set of statements again and again. To do this, iterative control structures called loops are used. In other words, loops are used to repeat a specific block of code.

Python provides two loops for iteration purposes. We will look at each one of these. Loops, just like decision making structures represent a block of code and all the statements within a loop should be a tab-space indent.

6.2.1 while Loop

A while loop executes all the statements under it as the given condition evaluates to True. General Syntax:

```
while (<condition>):
Statement 1
Statement 2
...
```

Example:

```
x = 0
while ( x < 10 ):
print x
x = x + 1
```

In this example, variable x has been initialized to 0. The condition given to the ***while loop*** is x < 10. As long as this condition is satisfied, the statements under the loop will be repeatedly executed. Logically, the statements under this loop print the value of x and also increment the value of x. This block of code will print values from 0 to 9. Once x becomes 10, the condition x < 10 will evaluate to false and the statements under the loop will no longer be executed.

Using *else* statement with a while loop:

It is possible to use ***else*** statement with a ***while loop***. The ***else*** code block will get executed when the condition of the ***while loop*** becomes false. General Syntax:

while (<condition>):

Statement 1

Statement 2

...

else:

Statements...

Even if, the ***while*** condition evaluates to False during the first check and no statements under the loop get executed, the ***else*** block will get executed. There are a few sample programs included at the end of this chapter which demonstrate the usage of control structures. Things will be clearer once you go through those programs.

6.2.2 for Loop

A for loop is used to iterate over items in a sequence such as string, list, tuple or dictionary. In a string, the loop iterates over each alphabet, in lists and tuples over each item and in a dictionary over each key. General Syntax:

for <iterating variable> in <sequence>:

Statement 1

Statement 2

...

Example 1:

str = "Hello"

for alphabet in str:

print "Current alphabet: ", alphabet

In Example 1, the variable ***str*** contains the string ***"Hello"***. The ***for loop*** uses an iterating variable ***alphabet*** to iterate through ***str***. During each iteration, the variable ***alphabet*** will hold each character from the string ***str***, starting from ***'H'*** to ***'o'***. As long as ***str*** is being iterated, the statements inside the ***for loop*** will be executed.

Example 2:

cities = ["Miami", "Tokyo", "Beijing", "Vancouver"]

for city in cities:

print city

In Example 2, the variable ***cities*** is a list which holds the names of 4 cities – ***"Miami", "Tokyo", "Beijing", "Vancouver"***. The iterating variable ***city*** inside the for loop will hold each of these city names from ***"Miami"*** to ***"Vancouver"*** during each iteration.

Using *else* statement with a *for* loop:

It is possible to use ***else*** statement with a for loop. The ***else*** code block will get executed when the loop has finished iterating through the given sequence. General Syntax:

for <iterating variable> in <sequence>:

Statements…

else:

Statements…

A script can have ***nested loops*** wherein a loop is present inside another loop. Example:

for <iterating variable> in <sequence>:

Statements…

while (<condition>):

Statements…

6.2.3 Loop Control

Loop control statements are used to alter the normal iterative process of a loop. These statements give better control to the programmer to handle certain conditions. The loop control statements are as follows:

6.2.3.1 Break Statement

This statement halts the execution of a loop and brings the execution control out of it. Consider a while loop used to print numbers from 1 to 5:

x = 1

while (x <= 5):

print x

x = x + 1

Say, we want to terminate the loop once x becomes 3. To do so, we incorporate the ***break statement*** as follows:

```
x = 1

while ( x <= 5 ):

print x

x = x + 1

if ( x == 3 ):

break
```

6.2.3.2 Continue Statement

This statement skips the remainder of the loop and goes back to check the condition before going ahead with the next iteration. Consider the for loop example (Example 1) from ***Section 6.2.2*** which prints each alphabet from a given string. Say, we want to avoid printing the alphabet "l". To do so, we incorporate the continue statement as follows:

```
str = "Hello"

for alphabet in str:

if ( alphabet == "l"):

continue

print "Current alphabet: ", alphabet
```

6.2.3.3 pass Statement

The ***pass statement*** is a null operation. It is required syntactically but does not have any significance otherwise, used when you do not want to do any operation. A ***pass statement*** will not make any alterations to the control of a loop.

6.3 Sample Programs

This section contains a few sample programs which demonstrate the usage of control structures. Writing and executing Python scripts have been explained in Section 3.

6.3.1 if-elif-else Combination

This program demonstrates the usage of ***if, elif*** and ***else*** statements. The scripts prompts the user to enter a number and determines whether the number is positive, negative or 0.

```
#Print a welcome message
print "This is if-elif-else demo...\n"
#Ask the user to enter a number, convert the string value
#Returned by raw_input to int using the int() function
x = int ( raw_input ( "Enter a number: " ))
#Check if x is -ve
if (x < 0) :
print "\n", x, "is a negative number.\n"
#Check if x is 0
elif ( x == 0):
print "\nThe entered number is zero.\n"
#If it is not negative and not zero, it is positive
else:
print "\n", x, "is a positive number.\n"
```

Output:

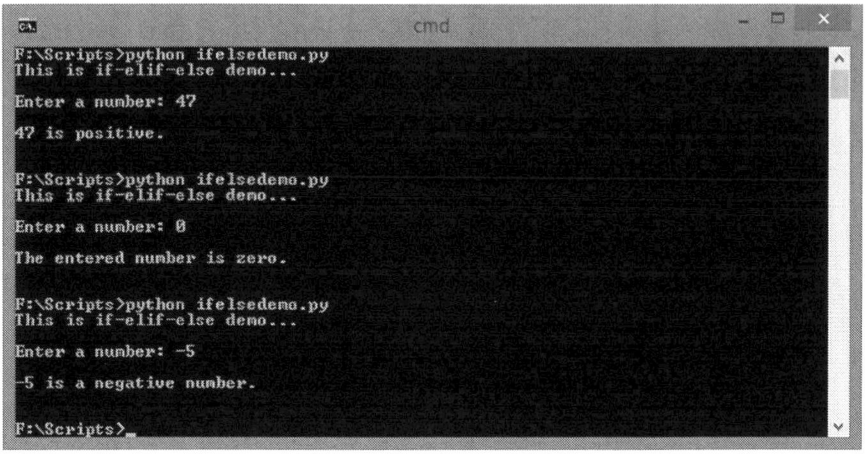

cmd
F:\Scripts>python ifelsedemo.py
This is if-elif-else demo...
Enter a number: 47
47 is positive.
F:\Scripts>python ifelsedemo.py
This is if-elif-else demo...
Enter a number: 0
The entered number is zero.
F:\Scripts>python ifelsedemo.py
This is if-elif-else demo...
Enter a number: -5
-5 is a negative number.
F:\Scripts>_

6.3.2 while Loop

This program demonstrates the usage of a ***while loop*** with the inclusion of ***else*** statement. The script prints numbers from 0 to 10. The variable ***x*** is initialized to ***0***. The ***while loop*** is only good enough to print the numbers from 0 to 9. When the condition (x < 10) evaluates to false, the ***else block*** gets executed.

```
#Print a welcome message on the screen
print "This is while loop demo...\n"
#Initialize x to 10
x = 0
#Loop as long as x is less than 10
while (x < 10):
#Print the value of x
print x
#Increment x
x = x + 1
#Once while condition (x < 10) evaluates to false
#i.e. x becomes greater than or equal to 10,
#this else block will be executed
else:
#Print the value of x
print x
```

Output:

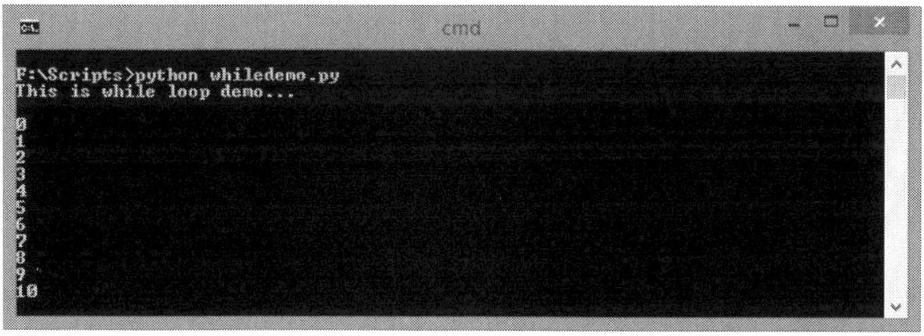
cmd
F:\Scripts>python whiledemo.py
This is while loop demo...
0
1
2
3
4
5
6
7
8
9
10

Chapter 7
Function Basics

A function is a block of reusable code that performs a specific task. In this sense, a function is a type of routine or procedure. Using functions in a script is good for modularity and code reusability. There are several built-in functions such as ***print, raw_input, type***, etc. It is also possible to define your own functions, also known as user-defined functions.

7.1 Defining a Function

A function represents a code block and hence all the statements under it should be indented by one tab-space indent. Here are syntax rules to define a function:

- A function block starts with the keyword ***def***, followed by the function name, parenthesis (( )) and a colon (:).
  - Eg. def some_function ():
- Any parameters that are passed to a function should be placed inside the parenthesis.
  - Eg. def some_function (x, y, z):
- The body of the function starts at one tab-space indent and can have an optional ***return*** statement. A return statement basically returns the execution control back to the calling function. The major use of a ***return*** statement is to return one or more variables, values or expressions back to the calling function.

return statement not returning any value is the same as ***return None***. If more than one variables, values or expressions are used to return, they need to be separated by a comma.

Putting all these rules together, the general syntax of defining a function looks like:

def <function_name>(<parameters>):

Statements…

return <optional variables, values or expressions>

Let us take a look at an example of function definition where in the function accepts two numbers as parameters and returns the sum:

def add (number1, number2):

sum = number1 + number2

return sum

7.2 Calling a Function

A function definition only defines what a function does but does not execute on its own. To execute a function, it should be called from somewhere else. To call a function, the following syntax is used:

<function_name> (<parameters>)

If a function is returning a value, it is best practice to store that value in a variable:

<variable> = <function_name> (<parameters>)

The variables passed to the function at the time of the function call are received in the same order as they are declared in the function definition.

For Example – Consider this function definition ***def <function_name> (<Parameter1>, <Parameter2>)*** and consider this call to the function – ***<function_name>(<Value1>, <Value2>)***. ***Parameter1*** will hold the value of ***Value1*** and ***Parameter2*** will hold the value of ***Value2*** respectively. Hence, while developing a script, the developer must consider the logical repercussions while setting the order of the parameters.

Let us go back to the ***add( )*** function defined in **Section 7.1** and see how it is called:

x = add (5, 10.5)

This function call passes numerical values of ***5*** and ***10.5*** to the function ***add( )***. The function starts executing according to its definition i.e. Accepts ***5*** and ***10.5*** as parameters ***number1 and number2 respectively***, adds them and returns their sum. This sum is then assigned to the variable ***x*** which is ***15.5***.

7.2.1 Returning Multiple Values

It is possible to return multiple values back to the calling function. The return statement should separate multiple values by a comma in the function definition and in the calling function, the variables accepting the returning values should be separated by a comma. This will perform multiple assignment of variables as explained in **Section 4**. Let us define and call a function which accepts two numbers and returns their sum, difference, and product.

```
#Function Definition
def calculator (number1, number2):
sum = number1 + number2
difference = number1 – number2
product = number1 * number2
return sum, difference, product
#Function Call
s, diff, prod = calculator (30, 10)
```

The function calculator returns 3 values – ***sum, difference*** and ***product***. These values will be assigned to ***s, diff*** and ***prod*** respectively. Multiple assignment will be performed over here.

Note: If a function accepts ***n*** number of parameters, exactly ***n*** number of arguments should be passed while making a function call else there will be an error. Default arguments make a partial exception to this rule which is covered in the sections to follow.

7.2.2 Keyword Arguments

Using keyword arguments, you can make a function call – manually passing the arguments to the function by setting the parameters. Parameters are identified by the same variable name as defined in the function definition. One advantage of using keyword arguments is that there is no need to follow the order of parameters.

Let us consider the following function definition:

def person (name, age, phone, address):

Statements…

A sample function call without using keyword arguments will require following of the order of paramcters as follows:

person("John", 30, 123456789, "New York")

Using keyword arguments, we can pass the arguments in any order as follows:

person(age = 30, address = "New York", name = "John", phone = 123456789)

7.2.3 Default Arguments

A default argument is a value assumed by a parameter if a particular argument is not given during a function call. This makes a partial exemption to the rule – number of arguments defined and passed should be the same. To set a default argument, the parameter in question is initialized to a value during function definition.

General Syntax:

def <function_name> (<parameter1> = <default_value1>):

Statements…

Example:

def University (name, address, rank = 0):

Statements…

We have defined a function called University which accepts 3 arguments – name, address, and rank with rank being the default argument. While making a function call, if the third argument is not supplied, a value of 0 will be assumed for rank. Consider the following calls:

University ("Melbourne University", "Australia", 5)

In this function call, we pass all 3 arguments. This will override the default value of rank and a value of 5 will be assigned to rank.

University ("XYZ University", "XYZ")

In this call, we just pass 2 arguments and no value of rank. In this case, 0 will be assigned for rank. It is a good idea to use Keyword Arguments while incorporating Default Arguments in your code as this promotes code readability and you do not have to remember the order.

Chapter 8
Programming Tutorials

This section covers step by step tutorials to write very basic programs.

8.1 Odd or Even

Divisibility by 2 is what determines whether a number is odd or even. In this tutorial, we will write a Python script to check if a number is odd or even. While zero is divisible by any number (including 2 and except 0), it may be considered as even but in the script, we will keep a special provision to check if it is 0.

We need to take input from the user, so we use ***raw_input*** function as follows:

num_str = raw_input("\nEnter a number: ")

Whatever the user enters will be stored in the variable ***num_str***. ***raw_input*** will always return a string and hence we will have to convert it to integer using the datatype conversion function ***int(str)*** as follows:

number = int(num_str)

First, we check if the number is zero. It is quite straightforward; we use the equal-to comparison operator as follows:

if (number == 0):

print "\nThe entered number is zero\n"

Then, we check its divisibility by 2 to find out if it is even. If the number is divisible by 2, the remainder should be 0. We make use of the modulus operator (%) to take the remainder and compare it with 0 with the equal-to comparison operator as follows:

elif (number % 2 == 0):

print "\nThe entered number: ", number , " is even\n"

If the number is not zero and if it is not divisible by 2, it means that the number is odd. To take care of this condition, we use the final else statement as follows:

else:

print "\nThe entered number: ", number , " is odd\n"

Putting it all together, we have the following code:

```
#Print welcome message on the screen
print "This Python Script checks if a given number is
odd or even\n"
#Wait for user input, retrieve it in a variable
num_str = raw_input("\nEnter a number: ")
#Convert the string input to int
number = int(num_str)
#Check if the number is zero
if (number == 0):
print "\nThe entered number is zero\n"
#Check if the number is divisible by 2, which would mean
it is even
elif ( number % 2 == 0):
print "\nThe entered number: ", number , " is even\n"
#If the number is not zero and it is not divisible by 2,
it would mean that it is odd
else:
print "\nThe entered number: ", number , " is odd\n"
```

8.2 Factorial

In this tutorial, we will write a Python script to accept a number from the user as input and calculate its factorial. A factorial of a non-negative integer ***n***, denoted by ***n!*** is the product of all the positive integers less than or equal to n, for example –> *5! = 120*. The general formula is ***n! = n x (n – 1)!*** and *0!* ***is*** *1*.

To start with the script, we will need to take the input from the user. We do this with the ***raw_input*** function as follows:

```
num_str = raw_input("\nEnter a number: ")
```

Whatever the user enters will be stored in the variable ***num_str***. ***raw_input*** will always return a string and hence we will have to convert it to integer using the datatype conversion function ***int(str)*** as follows:

```
number = int(num_str)
```

The result will be stored in the variable number which could be negative, zero or positive. If negative, we have to tell the user that factorials can be calculated for non-negative integers only. If zero, we need to tell the user that the factorial is 1 and if it is positive, we need to go about the actual calculations. The decision making is done as follows:

```
if (number < 0):

print "\nFactorial can only be calculated if a whole number.\n"

elif (number == 0):

print "Factorial of " + num_str + " is 1\n"

else:

#....FACTORIAL CALCULATIONS HERE....
```

In order to calculate the factorial of a positive integer, we will need a variable initialized to 1 which will keep track of products of all the integers starting from 1 till the input number. The variable we will use is ***factorial = 1***. A loop is needed to iterate from 1 to the input number. A ***for*** loop will do just that. Range function is used to return a list of numbers from 1 to the input number.

factorial = 1

for i in range(1, number + 1):

*factorial = factorial * i*

Putting it all together, we have the following code:

```
#Print welcome message on the screen
print "This Python Script calculates the factorial of a given number.\n"
#Wait for user input, retieve it in a variable
num_str = raw_input("\nEnter a number: ")
#Convert the string input to int
number = int(num_str)
#Check if the number is negative
if (number < 0):
print "\nFactorial can only be calculated of a whole number.\n"
#Check if the number is 0
elif (number == 0):
print "Factorial of " + num_str + " is 1\n"
#If the number is not 0 or negative, it implies that it is positive
else:
#Initialize factorial variable to 1
factorial = 1
#For loop, iterating i from 1 to the input number
for i in range(1, number + 1):
#Keep multiplying i to the factorial variable and asign it back to it
factorial = factorial * i
#Print factorial
print "Factorial of " + num_str + " is " , factorial
```

8.3 Reverse a number

In this tutorial, we will learn to write a Python script which reverses a given number.

We need to take input from the user, so we use ***raw_input*** function as follows:

num_str = raw_input("\nEnter a number: ")

Whatever the user enters will be stored in the variable ***num_str***. ***raw_input*** will always return a string and hence we will have to convert it to integer using the datatype conversion function ***int(str)*** as follows:

number = int(num_str)

A variable called reverse will be used to store the ***reverse*** of a given number, we initialize it to ***0*** as it will be used in a loop. We use ***while loop*** to iterate through the number. During each iteration, we take the last digit of the number by taking the ***Modulus 10 (number % 10)*** of it and adding it to ***reverse x 10***. Multiplying by 10 shifts the number to the left by one's place and this gives a chance to accommodate all the digits in reverse. Once we make use of the last digit, we no longer need it so we just truncate it by dividing the ***number by 10***. This will eventually make the number ***0*** which will help in negating the condition for the while loop.

while (number):

*reverse = reverse * 10 + (number % 10)*

number = number / 10

In the end, if you want to print the original ***number***, remember to use the ***num_str*** variable and not the number variable as the data in latter will no longer be available as a result of progressive division by 10.

We have the following code after putting all the concepts together:

```
#Print welcome message on the screen
print "This Python Script reverses a given number\n"
#Wait for user input, retieve it in a variable
num_str = raw_input("\nEnter a number: ")
#Convert the string input to int
number = int(num_str)
#Initialize a variable to 0 for storing the reverse of
a number
reverse = 0
#Iterate using while loop until number has a positive
value
while (number):
'''
In each iteration, get the last digit of the number by
taking number % 10
Add it to reverse * 10
'''
reverse = reverse * 10 + (number % 10)
#Get rid of the last digit once it is used by dividing
by 10
number = number / 10
'''
Print the reverse, num_str is used to print the original
input as the
Data in number is lost as a result of division
'''
print "The reverse of ", num_str , "is: ", reverse
```

8.4 String Palindrome

In this tutorial, we will write a Python script to check whether a given string is a Palindrome. A string which is the same as the original string when reversed is known as a palindrome. The logic to implement this script is pretty straightforward – reverse the string and check if it is the same as the original one.

We ask the user to input a string using the ***raw_input*** function and store the data in a variable as follows:

user_str = raw_input("\nEnter a string: ")

Length of the string is retrieved using the ***len()*** function. We will need the length while iterating in the loop:

length = len(user_str)

The variable which will hold the reverse of the original string is initialized:

reverse = ""

String reversal process is started with the help of a for loop, iterating it from ***(length – 1) to 0***. To do this, we use the range function – ***range (length – 1 , -1 , -1)***. This will return a list of numbers from ***(length – 1) to 0***. The first character in a string is at index ***0*** and the last one is at ***(length – 1)***. During each iteration, we concatenate each character of the input string from the last character to the first one to the variable reverse.

for i in range (length - 1 , - 1, -1):

reverse = str(reverse) + user_str[i]

reverse will now hold the reverse of the original string held in ***user_str*** variable. To check if the original string is a palindrome, we compare it with reverse as follows:

if (user_str == reverse):

print "\nThe given string: ", user_str , "is a palindrome\nReverse: ", reverse

else:

print "\nThe given string: ", user_str , "is not a palindrome\nReverse: ", reverse

Putting all the concepts together, we have the following code:

```
#Print welcome message on the screen
print "This Python Script checks if a given string is a palindrome.\n"
#Wait for user input, retieve it in a variable
user_str = raw_input("\nEnter a string: ")
#Get the length of the string using the len() function
length = len(user_str)
#Initialize reverse variable to ""
reverse = ""
#Reverse the string, iterate from length - 1 to 0
for i in range (length - 1 , - 1, -1):
#Keep adding characters from last index to 0, one by one
reverse = str(reverse) + user_str[i]
#Check if the input string and its reverse are equal
if (user_str == reverse):
print "\nThe given string: ", user_str , "is a palindrome\nReverse: ", reverse

else:
print "\nThe given string: ", user_str , "is not a palindrome\nReverse: ", reverse
```

8.5 Menu Driven Program using User Defined Functions

In this tutorial, we will learn to write a menu driven program to perform various arithmetic operations – addition, subtraction, multiplication, division, modulus, exponent and floor division. We will write User Defined functions to perform each of these operations. In the main code, we will display a menu repeatedly until the user wants to quit. This program combines the use of user input, control structure, and functions.

Let us start by defining the required functions. Writing user-defined functions and how they work has been explained extensively in **Section 7**. All the arithmetic functions have similar code with very little changes, hence only one will be explained which will serve as a template for the rest.

A function to add two numbers is defined as follows, it accepts 2 arguments – ***a*** and ***b***, calculates their sum and assigns it to a variable called ***sum*** and returns it.

def add(a, b):

sum = a + b

return sum

A dedicated function to accept and return 2 variables is written as there are several points in the program where user input will be required. Writing input statements, again and again, will bloat up the code. This is a classic example of code reusability. The function definition is as follows:

```
def takeinput():
a = raw_input("\nEnter a: ")
b = raw_input("\nEnter b: ")
return int(a), int(b)
```

In the main code, we display a menu repeatedly using a while loop and ask user to enter the choice. We use a variable called ***choice*** to store what user has entered. If choice is 1, addition is performed, if 2, subtraction is performed and so on. If choice is 0, the program quits – ***break*** statement is used to come out of the while loop.

```
choice = 99
while ( choice != 0 ):
choice_str = raw_input("\n1. Addition\n2. Subtraction\n3. Multiplication\n4. Division\n5. Exponent\n6. Floor Division\n7. Modulus\n0. Quit\nChoice: ")
choice = int (choice_str)
if ( choice == 1):
a, b = takeinput()
sum = add(a , b)
print "\nThe sum is: ", sum
elif ( choice == 2):
a, b = takeinput()
```

value = subtract(a , b)

print "\nThe value is: ", value

There are 8 option, 1-7 for performing arithmetic operations and 0 for quitting. It is important that choice variable holds none of these values and hence it has been ***initialized to 99*** before entering the while loop. ***raw_input*** function is used to display the menu and wait for user's input. This is accepted in the variable ***choice_str*** and then converted to integer and stored in the variable ***choice***. Then follow a bunch of ***if-elif-else*** combination statements which take appropriate action based on the value of ***choice***. Putting it all together, we have the following code:

```
#This script demonstrates the usage of functions

#Addition
def add(a, b):
#Add both values
sum = a + b
#Return sum to the calling functions
return sum

#Subtraction
def subtract(a, b):
#Subtract both values
value = a - b
#Return value to the calling functions
return value

#Multiplication
def multiply(a, b):
#Multiply both values
product = a * b
#Return product to the calling functions
return product

#Division
```

```
def divide(a, b):
#Divide both values
quotient = a / b
#Return quotient to the calling functions
return quotient

#Exponent
def exponent(a, b):
#Raise exponential power of the first operand by the
second
value = a ** b
#Return value to the calling functions
return value


#Floor Division
def floordivide(a, b):
#Floor-divide both values
quotient = a // b
#Return quotient to the calling functions
return quotient

#Modulus
def modulus(a, b):
#Take modulus
remainder = a % b
#Return remainder to the calling functions
return remainder
#Take inputs
def takeinput():
#Prompt user to enter a and b
a = raw_input("\nEnter a: ")
b = raw_input("\nEnter b: ")
#Return a and b in integer format
return int(a), int(b)

#Execution starts here. Print welcome message on the
screen
print "This is a menu driven script which performs
arithmetic operations with the help of functions.\n"
#This variable will be used to store user's choice
choice = 99
```

```
#Loop until choice is not equal to zero
while ( choice != 0 ):
#Prompt user to make a selection by displaying a menu
choice_str = raw_input("\n1. Addition\n2. Subtraction\n3. Multiplication\n4. Division\n5. Exponent\n6. Floor Division\n7. Modulus\n0. Quit\nChoice: ")
#Convert choice to integer
choice = int (choice_str)
#If choice is 1
if ( choice == 1):
a, b = takeinput()
sum = add(a , b)
print "\nThe sum is: ", sum
#If choice is 2
elif ( choice == 2):
a, b = takeinput()
value = subtract(a , b)
print "\nThe value is: ", value
#If choice is 3
elif ( choice == 3):
a, b = takeinput()
product = multiply(a , b)
print "\nThe product is: ", product
#If choice is 4
elif ( choice == 4):
a, b = takeinput()
quotient = divide(a , b)
print "\nThe quotient is: ", quotient
#If choice is 5
elif ( choice == 5):
a, b = takeinput()
value = exponent(a , b)
print "\nThe value is: ", value
#If choice is 6
elif ( choice == 6):
a, b = takeinput()
quotient = floordivide(a , b)
print "\nThe quotient is: ", quotient
#If choice is 7
elif ( choice == 7):
```

```
a, b = takeinput()
remainder = modulus(a , b)
print "\nThe remainder is: ", remainder
#If choice is 0
elif ( choice == 0):
print "\nQuitting...\n"
break
else:
#If a valid input is not entered.
print "\nInvalid option.\n"
```

Chapter 9
Final Words

This book gives you a very basic understanding of Python. Some concepts are understood better practically as opposed to theoretically. What cannot be explained theoretically has been explained in **Section 8** which deals with step by step tutorials of writing Python scripts. Being a general-purpose language, the scope and applications of Python are myriad.

Those considering a career in Python should explore more after reading and understanding the book. There are innumerable Python resources available on the web. Some of the more advanced topics in Python are – Classes and Objects, File I/O, Exception Handling, Web Programming, GUI Programming, etc. To be a professional programmer, some understanding of system internals is required and knowledge of C/C++ programming languages would help a great deal in pursuing a career in Python. Those interested in Web Programming in Python should have basic knowledge of HTML(5), CSS, JavaScript and Web Servers.

Good Luck & God Bless.

70240143R00049

Made in the USA
San Bernardino, CA
26 February 2018